My First Riddle

Puzzles In Poetry

Edited by Jonathan Fisher

First published in Great Britain in 2011 by:

 Young**Writers**

Remus House
Coltsfoot Drive
Peterborough
PE2 9BF
Telephone: 01733 890066
Website: www.youngwriters.co.uk

Foreword

'My First Riddle' was a competition specifically designed for Key Stage 1 children. The simple, fun form of the riddle gives even the youngest and least confident writers the chance to become interested in poetry by giving them a framework within which to shape their ideas. As well as this it also allows older children to let their creativity flow as much as possible, encouraging the use of simile and descriptive language.

Given the young age of the entrants, we have tried to include as many poems as possible. We believe that seeing their work in print will inspire a love of reading and writing and give these young poets the confidence to develop their skills in the future.

Our defining aim at Young Writers is to foster the talent of the next generation of authors. We are proud to present this latest collection of anthologies and hope you agree that they are an excellent showcase of young writing talent.

Contents

Langley Moor Primary School, Langley Moor

Launceston CP School, Launceston

Lingfield Notre Dame School, Lingfield

Marden Primary School, Marden

The Poems

Do I Have The X Factor?

Her hair is shiny and her skin is soft.
Her eyes are brown and sparkly.
Her lips are redder than cherries.
Her teeth are whiter than snow.
She is petite and dainty.
She is Cheryl Cole.

Hannah Fitzgerald (6)
Abbots Langley School, Abbots Langley

What Am I?

They are grey with horns
But not when they are born.
They are tough and strong
And they really do pong.

Harry Applin (6)
Abbots Langley School, Abbots Langley

Sweet Treat

What do children love to eat,
But Ghostbusters think it's no treat?
Stay Puft Marshmallow Man.

Darryl Barr (6)
Abbots Langley School, Abbots Langley

Who Am I?

I'm a female.
I'm an actress.
Who am I?
You might have seen me in a children's comedy.
In one I care for children,
In another I deal with a mean brother.
Who am I?
I'm funny and I am in Tracy Beaker.
People think I have long hair and I'm kind.
I act in Dani's House.
Dani Harmer.

Shyana Gobiraj (7)
Abbots Langley School, Abbots Langley

I Love My Guinea Pigs

Pippy and Sunny are nice and fluffy,
They squeak all day and are really very funny.
They have no tail but have tiny little ears,
Bigger than a hamster but smaller than a deer.
They like lots of cuddles but
Don't like going in muddy puddles.
Who are they?

Abigail Dolente (6)
Abbots Langley School, Abbots Langley

Pet Giraffe

I would like a pet giraffe,
Its skinny legs make me laugh.
It has a long neck and is very tall,
Next to it I would feel so small.
It has a long tongue to eat leaves.
'Mum can I have a giraffe please?'

Eveline Bolt (7)
Abbots Langley School, Abbots Langley

Untitled

I like playing with my yellow ball.
I have black and white patches.
I run as fast as a cheetah.
I am furry and fluffy as a kitten.
I am Murphy, the sheep dog.

Miles Pyatt (6)
Abbots Langley School, Abbots Langley

Nibbles

He's cute and cuddly but you cannot train him.
You'll get all muddy when you try to catch him.
All that squeaking, tweeting and chattering
Means he is hungry and won't stop munching.
Nibbles is my funny pet, I will always be there for him.
What is he?

Natasha Gatsky (6)
Abbots Langley School, Abbots Langley

Who Am I?

It is small and fluffy
It is lovely and cute
It likes to hide in my daddy's boot!

Its little nose is pink and soft
It likes to play lots
And can climb up to the loft!

It has a long tail and purrs lots
And sleeps on my bed
I like to stroke his warm head.

Ella Tomlin (6)
Abbots Langley School, Abbots Langley

A New Pet

This pet is sparkly and it's very, very small
It likes to move a lot
And I don't think it sleeps at all.

Jago Rowe (6)
Abbots Langley School, Abbots Langley

A Dog Called Sevvy

I know a pet called Sevvy
He is cute and really heavy
He has pointy ears and a long waggy tail.
And when he chases the ball
He is happy and a bit zappy!
He licks me all over and is really cool
And I love to see him at my school.

Joseph Geard (6)
Abbots Langley School, Abbots Langley

What Am I?

I am tall but I don't have leaves, but I may eat them.
I am grey but I can also be brown at times.
I have a trunk but no roots
But I may lift them from time to time.
What am I?

Elena Braddick Wood (6)
Abbots Langley School, Abbots Langley

Who Am I?

He has brown eyes and brown hair
And he likes to sing everywhere.
He's famous and a singer and he likes to dance.
He's thin or slim.
He's a young boy.
He won a trophy for best newcomer.
He wears a black jacket a lot.
He's finding somebody to love.

Taj Kapoor (6)
Abbots Langley School, Abbots Langley

My Team

He plays in blue
Top of the league
For you and me
That's Chelsea.

Kieran Burt (6)
Abbots Langley School, Abbots Langley

7

Aye-Aye

It is my favourite creature
It has two sharp teeth - with which to eat ya!
It has a long spindly finger
And a big bushy tail,
Ears like a bat's
And its eyes never fail.

The Aye-Aye is my favourite creature
Oh dear Aye-Aye how I'd love to meet ya!

Ben Culpeck (7)
Abbots Langley School, Abbots Langley

Big X Factor Judge's Friend

She has beautiful long brown hair
And sits as a judge on a chair
She sings songs I like
About having a fight
And is always on telly
But she doesn't have a big belly
Her friends are Simon Cowell and Louis Walsh
Her eye lashes are very false
Sharon Osbourne did her job but they sacked her
Now she's the face of X Factor
She also works for L'Oréal because she is a gorgeous looking girl.

Ella Broomfield (6)
Abbots Langley School, Abbots Langley

Cat In The Hat

He is an undressed grey cat.
Who wears a tall stripy hat.
He wears a red bow tie.
He goes flying in the sky.
He has a thingamajigger and a fish in his bowl.
Thing 1 and Thing 2 go travelling too.
The thingamajigger that goes smaller and bigger
It turns into a submarine.
He is the liveliest cat I have ever seen.

Emily Stewart (6)
Abbots Langley School, Abbots Langley

My Puffer Fish

He is fat.
He is spiky.
He is sharp.
He is hungry.

He wants to eat urchins.
He wants to eat shellfish.
He wants to eat crabs.
All on his dish.

Nikhil Roy (6)
Abbots Langley School, Abbots Langley

Cool Singer

He is 16.
He is a cute singer with brown eyes and brown hair.
His songs are fabulous.
My best songs are Baby and Favourite Girls,
Because they make me want to dance.
He can sing, play music on the piano, guitar and drums, that is so cool.
That is why girls love him.

Shantani Jepson (6)
Abbots Langley School, Abbots Langley

My Pet Hamster

I have a cheeky hamster
And she bites me very, very hard
And she likes to slurp her food.
She eats a lot of food.
She makes me laugh.
She lifts her bed outside her cage.
She climbs on the bars at the top of the cage and runs on her wheel.
Can you guess her name?

Grace Dowding (6)
Abbots Langley School, Abbots Langley

Frank Lampard

He's strong
He's quick
He's skilful on the pitch
He's great
He's cool
He's brilliant at football
He plays for Chelsea and England.
He is Frank Lampard.

Alfie Marriott (6)
Abbots Langley School, Abbots Langley

My Friend

My friend is soft with a rumbly tummy
He is naughty and very funny.
He bounces around when I gave him his breakfast and tea
And when we let him out he is very lively.
Have you guessed who it is yet?

Alice Tucker (6)
Abbots Langley School, Abbots Langley

The Best Band

This is the best band,
And I am their biggest fan
They sing, dance and act in a movie,
With their little brother Frankie.
Their names are Nick, Kevin and Joe.
And all together they are Jobro.
Who am I?

Niamh Kew (6)
Abbots Langley School, Abbots Langley

The Jungle

I am stripy
My colours are black and orange
I have whiskers like a cat
I roar and I hunt
I eat other animals for my dinner
I live in the jungle
What am I?

Anna Norris (6)
Abbots Langley School, Abbots Langley

Andrew

He runs as fast as a cheetah.
He is as funny as a frog.
He is as happy as a hyena.
He is as cool as Ben 10.
We play like best friends.
He is my friend, Andrew.

Jake Stewart (6)
Abbots Langley School, Abbots Langley

The Monkey

I live in the jungle.
I'm usually brown.
I have got a long tail
And I like to swing in the trees.
I like bananas and you won't find me on the ground.

Andrew Bell (6)
Abbots Langley School, Abbots Langley

Twinkle

I have soft warm fur
And a little twitching nose
I have big strong teeth
You can stroke my long fluffy ears
I have a lucky foot
And a fluffy white tail
I am Hannah's pet.
Who am I?

Hannah Brown (6)
Abbots Langley School, Abbots Langley

What Am I?

I'm black and white.
I take a bite.
Then splash out of sight.
I am a killer whale.

Jamie Hanlon (6)
Abbots Langley School, Abbots Langley

14

What Is It?

It likes to eat worms
It lays eggs
Some animals like to eat it
Some are big
Some are small
It likes to fly
In the sky
It is covered in feathers
And it is nice and soft
What is it?

Naheedah Khatun (6)
Abbots Langley School, Abbots Langley

Zebra

I am stripy black and white.
Also friendly and not so light.
I am large and quite tall.
As well as having a swishy tail.

Elise Wylie (6)
Abbots Langley School, Abbots Langley

A Riddle About Something Pink

This is pink
Sometimes it stinks
It likes to wiggle
May is its special month
It used to be a lump
It eats sloppy foods
It often coos
It sometimes smiles
More than once in a while
It likes to sleep
And it hardly ever weeps.
What is it?
Florence – my baby sister.

Jacob Bruguier (7)
Abbots Langley School, Abbots Langley

My Furry Friend

She is black and hairy
Sometimes she tries to be scary
She is always happy
But she is sometimes snappy
She is cheeky and greedy and a pest
I love her, she is the best.

Daisy Humphrey (6)
Abbots Langley School, Abbots Langley

My Mungo

I have travelled from Scotland.
My tail goes round like a helicopter when I wag it.
I am as black as the night sky.
I have got a scruffy beard.
I have got bushy eyebrows that wiggle when I blink.
My four legs are short and I wish I was bigger.
What am I?

George Hurdle (6)
Abbots Langley School, Abbots Langley

The Famous Footballer

He is talented at playing football.
He is famous all over the world.
He is English.
He is quick with the football.
He is fit because he trains a lot.
He is excellent at football.
He was a fantastic captain.
He is magnificent at corners and free kicks.
He is David Beckham.

Sam Tyler (6)
Abbots Langley School, Abbots Langley

17

My Best Friend

She is playful and fast
She will never come last
She will always be a friend
She will always be kind
She is smelly when wet
But the cutest thing I've met
She is black and white
And never uses a lead.

Jessica Dean (6)
Abbots Langley School, Abbots Langley

John Barrowman

I am tall
I am funny
I like dressing up for telly
My coat is full of sparkle
And my songs are too.
Who am I?

Charlie Bailey (6)
Abbots Langley School, Abbots Langley

My Brother

He's as caring as a fairy
He's as wonderful as a melted chocolate bar
He's brighter than a colourful flower
He is cuter than a kitten
He's as beautiful as a butterfly
He is more colourful than a butterfly
He is more helpful than a busy bee
He's as kind as a dog
He's funnier than a monkey
He's as amazing as a dog
He is greater than a pop star
He is softer than a furry kitten
He's as light as a cat
He's as fantastic as a flexible dog
He's as friendly as a bird
He is happier than a monkey
He's as crazy as a monkey
He's as tiny as a chair
He's as brilliant as a dog
He's as delicate as a cat
He's as ripe as a berry
He's as lovely as a kitten
And his name is Jack.

John Gibson (7)
Ashgrove Primary School, Carnmoney

My Best Friend

She's as funny as a clown.
She's as cute as a fluffy brown rabbit.
She's as soft as a caring squirrel.
She's as wonderful as the sun.
She's as lovely as a colourful butterfly.
She's as awesome as a rainbow.
She's as cool as a heart.
She's as amazing as a cuddly teddy.
She's as gentle as a rose.
She's as brilliant as a good listener.
She's as good as a diamond.
She's as interesting as yellow.
She's s thin as a flower.
She's as careful as me.
Her name is Molly.

Louise Dorman (7)
Ashgrove Primary School, Carnmoney

My Sister

She's as cute as a button
She's as funny as a clown
She's as silly as a squirrel
She's as kind as a fairy
She's as nice as summer
She's as fast as a cheetah
She's as pretty as a butterfly
She's as kind as a ladybird
She's as helpful as a bee
She's as thin as a stick
She's as lovely s a rose
She's as cuddly as a bear
She's as delicate as a bird.

Sophie Foster (7)
Ashgrove Primary School, Carnmoney

My Friend

He's as kind as a chicken.
He's as funny as Dilly.
He's as cute as a baby.
He's as weird as a bird.
He's as colourful as a peacock.
He's as shiny as a star.
He's as wonderful as a summer's day.
He's as bouncy as a trampoline.
He's as soft as a kitten.
He's as helpful as a busy bee.
He's as fast as a zebra.
He's as gentle as an elephant.
He's as caring as a dog.
He's my best friend Kyle.

Adam Dorrian (8)
Ashgrove Primary School, Carnmoney

My Cousin

She's as beautiful as a princess.
She's as wonderful as a chocolate bar.
She's as colourful as a rainbow.
She's as kind as your mum.
She's as helpful as a busy, busy bee.
She's as amazing as a tightrope walker.
She cares about everyone.
She's as musical as kind tweeting.
She's as grateful as the Lord Jesus.
She's as careful as an angel.
She's as fair as everyone.
She's as thankful as everyone.
She's as shiny as a shooting star.
She's more thoughtful than anyone.
She's the best cousin, and she's Nikita.

Jonathan O'Reilly (8)
Ashgrove Primary School, Carnmoney

21

Who Are We?

We are very, very selfish and jazzy.
Our clothes are pretty.
We have giant feet.
We live in a village.
You will recognise us with our curly hair.
We hate Cinderella and mice.
The ugly sisters.

Emma Martin (6)
Aston Lodge Primary School, Aston

Who Am I?

You may find me in a deep, dark wood in a ramshackle cottage.
At Christmas I am never seen, but you will see me lots at Halloween.
I may have a cat or bat but nothing else.
My hat is not to keep my head warm or cool, it is part of my uniform.
I have a broom, but it is not for sweeping.
With my magic wand I can turn you into a toad.
My cauldron is not used for cooking.
Can you guess who I am?
A wicked witch.

Rowan Danks (7)
Aston Lodge Primary School, Aston

Who Am I?

My hair is brown
I am very good
I grew a beanstalk
To climb and see the giant
I stole some chicken
I stole some golden eggs.
Jack.

Reece Weaver (6)
Aston Lodge Primary School, Aston

Who Am I?

I live in a pretty little cottage with my mother.
You can see me being kind and helpful.
I have lovely brown golden hair.
My favourite clothes are my long red cloak and my black shoes.
Sometimes I visit Granny and take my basket with gifts in for her.
When you see me the wolf will be following me.
Who am I?
Little Red Riding Hood.

Hannah Moore (6)
Aston Lodge Primary School, Aston

Who Am I?

I'm brilliant
I think I look beautiful
I live in a high place and sleep a lot
I get married to the prince
A prince kisses me to make me alive.
Who am I?

Caitlan Walker (6)
Aston Lodge Primary School, Aston

Who Am I?

I look very smart.
My behaviour is extremely good.
If you see me you will see my cosy fur.
I am tiny.
I live in the woods.
I'm annoyed because someone broke my chair.
I am baby bear.

Dillon Nicholls (7)
Aston Lodge Primary School, Aston

Who Am I?

My wooden cottage is in the woods.
I like to go out in the woods.
My dad is big and my mum is smaller.
I have soft fur.
I am sad because my chair is broken.
I am sad because my porridge is gone.
There was a little girl in my bed snoozing.
I am Baby Bear.

Izzy Williams, Connor Green, Nathan Haywood,
Anna Derbyshire, Andrew Morris & Leannder Cryer (6)
Aston Lodge Primary School, Aston

Mystery Guest

She is as white as a cloud.
She is as big as a basket.
She is as fluffy as cotton wool.
She has four legs.
She is as hoppy as a kangaroo.
She is Smudgey my rabbit.

Mia Coombs-Goodfellow (6)
Bel Royal Primary School, St Lawrence

Mystery Guest

He screams like bus brakes
He is as funny as a clown
He is as cute as a button
He is as lovely as a flower
He is as cheeky as a monkey
He is Lennox my brother.

Leyton Black (6)
Bel Royal Primary School, St Lawrence

Mystery Guest

She is as kind as a sweetheart
She is as cuddly as a pillow
She is as beautiful as a princess
She is as sweet as sweets
She is my mum and I love her.

Kyle Lilly (6)
Bel Royal Primary School, St Lawrence

Mystery Guest

She is as cute as a flower.
She is as fast as a turtle.

She is shiny as a star.
She eats like a rabbit.

She is Orange, my fish.

Amy Lloyd-Jones (6)
Bel Royal Primary School, St Lawrence

Mystery Guest

She is as happy as a duck.
She is as weird as a rhinoceros.
She is as funny as a monkey.
She is as crazy as a spider.
She is arty like a squiggly snail.
She is my mum and I love her.

Toby Ormsby (6)
Bel Royal Primary School, St Lawrence

27

Mystery Guest

He is as funny as a clown.
He is as black as soot.
He is as fast as roller skates.
He is strong like a tree.
He is my dad and I adore him.

Finlay Ormsby (6)
Bel Royal Primary School, St Lawrence

Mystery Guest

She can shout as loud as a giant
She is bossy like the Queen
She is kinder than her friends
Her hair is long like a ribbon
At parties she is as pretty as a princess
She is my mum and I love her.

Marley Siham (6)
Bel Royal Primary School, St Lawrence

Mystery Guest

He is cuddly like a bear
He is as fun as a school
He is as funny as a racing car
He is as clever as a scientist
He is as good looking as me
He is as fluffy as a hamster
He is my cat, Scruffy.

Ronaldo Rodrigues (6)
Bel Royal Primary School, St Lawrence

Mystery Guest

He is as fluffy as a horse
He is as silly as a clown
He is as cute as a baby
He is as big as a cat
He is Hoopy my rabbit.

Liam Oury (6)
Bel Royal Primary School, St Lawrence

Mystery Guest

She is as funny as a monkey
She is as cute as a flower
She is as silly as an elephant
She is as loud as a tiger
She pulls hair as hard as a gorilla
She is Michaela, my sister and I love her.

Abby McHugh (6)
Bel Royal Primary School, St Lawrence

Sollie Sambo

She is as soft as a butterfly
She is as sharp as a bear
She is as cuddly as a teddy bear
She is as black as a bat
She is as fast as a cheetah
She is Sollie Sambo, my dog.

Emily Johnson (5)
Burneston CE Primary School, Burneston

Buster, My Dog

He is as soft as a feather
He is as tall as a chair
He is as fast as a horse
He is as lovely as a friend
He is Buster, my dog.

Grace Clayton (6)
Burneston CE Primary School, Burneston

Rose

She is as kind as a cat
She is as beautiful as a butterfly
She is as cuddly as a cat
She is as sweet as a lollipop
She is as cheeky as a chimpanzee
She is Rose, my hamster.

Daisy Wesson (5)
Burneston CE Primary School, Burneston

Marcus

He is as fast as a cheetah
He is as little as a mouse
He is as handsome as a prince
He is as funny as a clown
He is as happy as the sun
He is as strong as a rock
He is as cute as a puppy
He is Marcus, my friend.

Owen Allsopp (6)
Burneston CE Primary School, Burneston

Untitled

He is as lazy as a cat.
He is as fast as a cheetah.
He is as cool as James Bond.
He is as handsome as a prince.
He is as cute as a baby.
He is as white as a cloud.
He is as fat as a pig.
He is as small as a mouse.
He is Scooby, my hamster.

Joe Hodgkinson (6)
Burneston CE Primary School, Burneston

Lily

She is as cute as a cat.
She is as funny as a monkey.
She is as happy as a coconut.
She is as selfish as the sun.
She is Lily, my sister.

Mia Barnett (5)
Burneston CE Primary School, Burneston

Bruce

He is as chubby as a lettuce.
He is as spotty as a Dalmatian.
He is as cheeky as a monkey.
He is as small as a mouse.
He is as naughty as an elephant.
He is as cuddly as a teddy bear.
He is as funny as a clown.
He is as cute as a kitten.
He is as handsome as a prince.
He is Bruce, my rabbit.

Lucy Clarke (6)
Burneston CE Primary School, Burneston

Izzy

She is as cuddly as a feather
She is patterned like a tortoise
She is as cheeky as a cheetah
She is as fluffy as a rabbit
She is lovely like Mum
She is Izzy, my kitten.

Jodie Yeatman (5)
Burneston CE Primary School, Burneston

My Mum

She is as cuddly as a cat.
She is as lovely as a teacher.
She is as nice as a friend.
She is as trusting as a pupil.

Daniel Radin (6)
Burneston CE Primary School, Burneston

Amber

She is as cheeky as a monkey.
She is as cuddly as a teddy.
She has sharp teeth like a shark.
She is as golden as sand.
She is as naughty as a lion.
She is Amber, my dog.

Liberty Barnett (5)
Burneston CE Primary School, Burneston

Molly

She is as clever as a computer.
She is as good as a musician.
She is as white as paper.
She is as smooth as cotton wool.
She is as cute as a baby kitten.
She is Molly, my dog.

Polly Stones (5)
Burneston CE Primary School, Burneston

Zac

He is as friendly as a friend.
He is as gorgeous as a prince.
He is as cute as a kitten.
He is as soft as a cushion.
He is Zac, my cat.

Amy Lee (5)
Burneston CE Primary School, Burneston

Josh

He is as funny as a clown.
He is as helpful as a doctor.
He is as cute as Steven Gerrard.
He is as fast as a cheetah.
He is as nice as my teddy.
He is as naughty as a baby.
He is Joshie, my brother.

Sammy Rowley (6)
Burneston CE Primary School, Burneston

Cass

He is as hairy as a monkey.
He is as jumpy as a trampoline.
He is as brown as a tree trunk.
He is as cute as a cat.
H is as fast as a cheetah.
He is as scratchy as a mouse.
He is Cass, my dog.

Kai Garner (5)
Burneston CE Primary School, Burneston

Panda

It is as black and white as a zebra.
Its claws are s sharp as a bear.
It is as fluffy as a cloud.
It is as slow as a tortoise.
It is as cute as a puppy.
It is a panda.

Richard Pulman (6)
Burneston CE Primary School, Burneston

Barney

He is as fast as a cheetah.
He is as black as a blackbird.
He is as funny as a clown.
He is as cheeky as a monkey.
He is as soft as a cushion.
His teeth are sharper than tigers.
He is as good as gold.
He is as smart as my school uniform.
He is as handsome as a prince.
He is Barney, my puppy.

Charlotte Hutchinson (6)
Burneston CE Primary School, Burneston

Maisie Mouse

It is as cute as a teddy
It is as fluffy as a feather
It is as fast as a cheetah
It is as beautiful as a princess
It is as cuddly as a teddy bear
It is Maisie Mouse, my cat.

Betty Brown (5)
Burneston CE Primary School, Burneston

Golden Eagle

It hunts like a tiger
It is as quiet as a feather
It is as smooth as a fish
It is as quiet as a mouse
It is as fast as a cheetah
Its golden feathers are like a sunset
It soars like a plane
It is a golden eagle.

Louis Schofield (7)
Burneston CE Primary School, Burneston

Mia

She is as nice as a sunflower.
She is as beautiful as a butterfly.
She is as cheeky as a monkey.
She is as good as gold.
She is as cute as a kitten.
She is Mia, my friend.

Kiera Greasley (6)
Burneston CE Primary School, Burneston

Rocket

He is as cuddly as my mummy and daddy.
He is as kind as my friends.
He is as fast as me.
He is as soft as a teddy.
He is as black as night.
He is as sleepy as me.
His teeth are as sharp s a shark.
He is Rocket, my cat.

Millie Harford (5)
Burneston CE Primary School, Burneston

A Football Star

He is as fast as a car.
He is as clever as God.
He is as strong as a gorilla.
He is as popular as a rock star.
He is as cool as a cat.
He is as clever as a scientist.
He is as small as a mouse.
He is as nice as a teacher.
He is Messi the football player.

Samuel Southgate (6)
Cedars Park Community Primary School, Stowmarket

My Cat

He is as nice as a flower.
He is as cute as a bunny.
He is as fast as a cheetah.
He is as cuddly as a teddy.
He is as cheeky as a monkey.
He is as soft as a feather.
He is a cat called Jake.

Lily Allum (6)
Cedars Park Community Primary School, Stowmarket

My Hamster

She is as sweet as a cat.
She is as small as a mouse.
She is as good as a guinea pig.
She is as fast as a cheetah.
She is as soft as a dog.
She is as noisy as an owl.
She is as dozy as a bat in the day.
She is my hamster, Rosey.

Alysha Walker (6)
Cedars Park Community Primary School, Stowmarket

My Hamster

He is as soft as a cat.
He is as white as cotton wool.
His eyes are black as gorillas.
He is as naughty as a monkey.
He is Hamie the hamster.

Keelan Winter (6)
Cedars Park Community Primary School, Stowmarket

Untitled

She is as sporty as Cameron.
She is as loving as a bunny.
She is as silly as a dog.
She is cuddly as a teddy bear.
She is funny as a cat.
She is mad as a bunny.
She is as fast as a sports car.
She is as bad as a bear.
She is a better dancer than Michael Jackson.
She is my guinea pig.

Katie Rogers (6)
Cedars Park Community Primary School, Stowmarket

My Dog

He is as happy as a bee.
He is as funny as a circus.
He is as quick as a cheetah.
He is as cool as a lion.
He is as famous as the Queen.
He is as sweet as honey.
He is my dog, Devon.

Oliver Fitzsimons (7)
Cedars Park Community Primary School, Stowmarket

Pop Star

She is a better singer than Michael Jackson.
She is as amazing as an acrobat show.
She's like a star.
She is a better dancer than Justin Beiber.
She is as pretty as a flower.
I think she is brilliant like my teddy bear.
I think she is fantastic like my family.
She is Hannah Montana.

Molly Pearce (6)
Cedars Park Community Primary School, Stowmarket

The Scarecrow

He is as light as a feather
He is as lovely as a flower
He is louder than my dad
He is as fast as a cheetah
He is as naughty as a gorilla
He is a king like Peter Pan
He is a nice friend
He is nice
He is a great footballer like Rio Ferdinand
He is a good swimmer
He is cute
He is as scary as a dinosaur
He can fly.

Harvey Talbot (5)
Cedars Park Community Primary School, Stowmarket

My Sister

She is as fast as a cheetah.
She jumps as high as a kangaroo.
She is as cheeky as a fox.
She is as cuddly as a bear.
She is as happy as my daddy.
She is as cute as a chinchilla.
She is Amelie my sister.

Ethan Harvey (6)
Cedars Park Community Primary School, Stowmarket

44

My Dog

He is as cheeky as a monkey.
He has teeth as sharp as a shark's.
He is as fast as a cheetah.
He is as greedy as a horse.
He is very loving like a family.
He is as cute as a rabbit.
He is as playful as a friend.
He is as smiley as a giraffe.
He is as small as a kitten.
He is as hoppy as a kangaroo.
He is as funny as a comedian.
He is as excited as a clown.
He is as noisy as an owl.
He is as soft as a bear.
He is as cheerful as a meerkat.
It is my dog, Brady.

Lukas Fishlock (6)
Cedars Park Community Primary School, Stowmarket

Fluffy The Rabbit

She is as naughty as a monkey,
She is as fluffy as a cushion,
She is fast like a person,
She is as funny as a clown,
She is Fluffy the rabbit.

Summer Mark (6)
Cedars Park Community Primary School, Stowmarket

My Dad

He is as strong as a giant.
He is as fast as a cheetah.
He is as good at football as David Beckham.
He is as big as a giant.
He is as hungry as a wolf.
As thirsty as a lion.
He is my dad.

Cameron Strachan (6)
Cedars Park Community Primary School, Stowmarket

My Cat

She is as fast as a cheetah.
She is as soft as a horse.
She is as sweet as sugar.
She is as good as a school boy.
She is as naughty as a lion.
She is Lottie the cat.

Tom Robinson (6)
Cedars Park Community Primary School, Stowmarket

My Dad

He is as big as a mountain.
And bad like thunder.
He is very silly, even sillier than a clown.
He is the best, better than the world.
He is so lazy, lazy like a cat.
He is my dad.

Ben Brown (7)
Cedars Park Community Primary School, Stowmarket

My Best Friend Ever

He is as cute as a puppy.
He is as funny as a clown.
He is as fluffy as a pillow.
His hair is dark gold.
His eyes are as blue as the sea.
He is Jamie, my best friend ever.

Ella Calver (6)
Cedars Park Community Primary School, Stowmarket

The Scarecrow

The scarecrow
She has got a hat
She is light as a feather
She is as sweet as a fox
She is as spiky as a crocodile
She is as cool as a cat
She is loud like a monster
She has a carrot nose.

Chloe Leeder (5)
Cedars Park Community Primary School, Stowmarket

Scarecrow

He is as scary as a ghost.
He is as prickly as my dad.
He wears a hat like my grandad.
He is as hard as a pumpkin.
He wears a jumper like my sister.
He is scared of the birds like me.
He is a scarecrow.

Emma Balaam (5)
Cedars Park Community Primary School, Stowmarket

The Scarecrow

The scarecrow
She has a bird on her hat
She has a tie
She has a blue coat
She's on grass
She's on sparkly grass
She has a carrot beak
She has black eyes
She has a peachy face
She has a smiley mouth
She has a black mouth.

Georgia Moore (5)
Cedars Park Community Primary School, Stowmarket

The Scarecrow

He is as nice as a hedgehog
He is as light as a feather
He is as nice as my dad
He is as nice as a dragon.

Oliver Doggett (5)
Cedars Park Community Primary School, Stowmarket

The Scarecrow

He is as scary as a dinosaur
He is as loud as a rock star
He is as spiky as a lizard
He is as great as my dad
He is my scarecrow.

Kody Emerick (5)
Cedars Park Community Primary School, Stowmarket

Scarecrow

He has a hat
He has a jacket
He has patterns on his jacket
He is scary as a hedgehog.

Caitlin Rookyard (5)
Cedars Park Community Primary School, Stowmarket

Scarecrow

He is lonely.
He wears a hat.
He is nicer than a horse.
He is big.
He is tied to a stick.

Leila Trueman (5)
Cedars Park Community Primary School, Stowmarket

Scarecrow

He is as smelly as a deer.
He is made of straw.
He is wearing a hat.
He is as scary as a crow.
He is as fat as a pumpkin.

Jack Atkins (5)
Cedars Park Community Primary School, Stowmarket

What Am I?

I have a very long neck to help me reach food high up in the trees.
My spots are orange that you can see.
My legs are medium-sized and very thin.
I rhyme with laugh.
What am I?

Ella Baldwin (6)
Copeland Road Primary School, West Auckland

What Am I?

I come in brown and I can climb 60 metres up a tree.
I love to eat bananas.
I swing from tree to tree.
I rhyme with funky.
What am I?

Daniel Paterson (7)
Copeland Road Primary School, West Auckland

What Am I?

I am very cute.
My fur is nice and warm.
When you're cold and you cuddle me, you'll be warm too.
As a treat, please give me a big juicy carrot.
I have whiskers and I live in a hutch.
What am I?

Emily Powton (6)
Copeland Road Primary School, West Auckland

What Am I?

I stuff my food into my cheeks.
I come out to play at night-time.
I might be black.
I live in a cage and I love to run on my wheel.
What am I?

Holly Simpson (7)
Copeland Road Primary School, West Auckland

What Am I?

I am a meat eater.
On my big body I have black and ginger little spots.
My legs are really strong.
When I see an enemy, I sneak through the long grass and lash out.
I mostly eat snakes.
I have really sharp teeth.
At night I can be nocturnal.
If I go backwards, I am an *aneyh*.

Jessica Maughan (6)
Copeland Road Primary School, West Auckland

What Am I?

I come in different breeds.
Sometimes I can run really fast.
I can slaver.
Sometimes I can bite.
I'm barking mad.
I rhyme with frog.
What am I?

Kieran Baldwin (6)
Copeland Road Primary School, West Auckland

What Am I?

I'm very small.
My home is in the grass.
As a very, very special treat . . .
I love a bit of lettuce.
I am extremely slow.
My shell is made of hexagonal shapes.
I am a greenish colour and I rhyme with porpoise.
What am I?

Charlie Jackson (6)
Copeland Road Primary School, West Auckland

What Am I?

I am very cute and furry.
My fur is very soft.
As for treats, a delicious chicken dinner please.
My fur is so soft - you can feel it.
I have pointy ears that are furry.
I have a cute nose that is pretty.
My tail is furry and cute but I might bark at you.
What am I?

Ella Appleby (6)
Copeland Road Primary School, West Auckland

Spider-Man

He is as smart as a hero.
He is as red as a cherry.
He is as tough as a wrestler.
He is Spider-man.

Jaafar Al-Khazraji (6)
Devonshire Primary School, Sutton

Johnny Depp

He is as rich as a rock star,
He is as funny as a clown,
He is as cool as a detective,
He is as famous as a book character,
He is a man,
He is Johnny Depp.

Yusuf Al-Unufi (6)
Devonshire Primary School, Sutton

Rocksea Cat

She is as bright as the sun
She is as white as the snow
She is as furry as a bear
She is as naughty as a monkey
She is my cat.

Leo Lemin (6)
Devonshire Primary School, Sutton

Steven Gerrard

He is as funny as a clown.
He is as bright as a monkey.
He is as cuddly as a teddy bear.
He is even faster than a cheetah.
He is as cool as a sports car.
He is Steven Gerrard.

Aditya Singh (6)
Devonshire Primary School, Sutton

Aaron Lennon

He is as fast as a cat.
He is more famous then Beckham.
He is skinnier than me.
He is as cool as an ice cream.
He is Aaron Lennon.

Ryan Robinson (6)
Devonshire Primary School, Sutton

My Friend Nayana

She's as wonderful as a bird
She's as cool as a rock star
She's as delicate as a butterfly
She's as kind as a queen
She's as cute as a baby
She's as pretty as a princess
She's as wise as an owl
She's as lovely as a fairy.

Saakshi Deshpande (6)
Devonshire Primary School, Sutton

My Best Friend Sarah

She's as energetic as a cheetah
She's as funny as a hyena
She's as kind as a bird
She's as talented as an acrobat
She's as cheerful as a chipmunk
She's Sarah, my best friend.

Rida Faisal (6)
Devonshire Primary School, Sutton

Percy Jackson

He's as active as a dog.
He's as heroic as a superhero.
He's as smart as a singer.
He's as cool as a rock star.
He's as energetic as a cheetah.
He's Percy Jackson.

Anirvinya Sood (6)
Devonshire Primary School, Sutton

My Friend Rida

She's as funny as a clown
She's as kind as my mum
She's as tall as a mountain
She's as clever as my dad
She's as smart as a queen
She's Rida.

Sarah Helps (7)
Devonshire Primary School, Sutton

Untitled

They are as fast as hamsters.
They are as greedy as a monkey.
They run like a pig.
They are black, white and brown like a gorilla.
They are my dogs, Bella and Charlie.

Keeley Purdy (5)
Haselbury Plucknett CE First School, Haselbury

Untitled

It is fast on slabs.
It is slow on stones.
It is black.
It has wheels.
It is my quad bike.

Connor Vincent (5)
Haselbury Plucknett CE First School, Haselbury

Untitled

It is as fast as a racing car.
It is as hot as a hot air balloon.
It is jet-packed like an aeroplane.
It lands on the moon like a satellite.
It is a rocket.

Lily Duckett (5)
Haselbury Plucknett CE First School, Haselbury

My Riddle

He is as cute as a puppy.
He is as super as Spider-Man.
He is as delicate as a vase.
He hops like a kangaroo.
He is as fast as a cheetah.
He is as cuddly as a teddy.
He scratches like a fox.
He is as colourful as a path.
He is as comfy as a chair.
It is my rabbit.

Thomas Lauchlan (6)
Haselbury Plucknett CE First School, Haselbury

Untitled

It is brown like a tree.
It glides like a bird.
It is fast like a cheetah.
It is cool like a racing car.
It is mean like a bear.
It is big like a house.
It is a golden eagle.

Ben Harris (5)
Haselbury Plucknett CE First School, Haselbury

Untitled

She is as red as fire.
She is as long as ruler.
She is as skinny as me.
She is as naughty as a gorilla.
She is as squashy as Nanny.
She is as cheeky as Mr Green.
She is orange like a basket.
She is my snake.

Katie Hooker (6)
Haselbury Plucknett CE First School, Haselbury

Untitled

She is as bossy as a cat.
She is as lovely as a cute kitten.
She is as nice as a mum.
She is as lovely as a princess.
She lives in a castle or a palace.
She is the Queen.

Sophie Loader (5)
Haselbury Plucknett CE First School, Haselbury

Untitled

It is as sharp as a sword.
It is as hot as fire.
It looks like a puffy cloud.
It is as hard as metal.
It is as big as a boat.
It is a rock at the beach.

Harrison Bennett (6)
Haselbury Plucknett CE First School, Haselbury

Untitled

He is as fast as a cheetah.
He is as small as a ball.
He is as funny as a clown.
He is as black as coal.
He has yellow eyes like a tiger.
He is as beautiful as a flower.
He is as fluffy as a feather.
He is my new kitten, Zulek.

Aniela Wodynska (6)
Haselbury Plucknett CE First School, Haselbury

Untitled

It smells like scent.
It is as wonderful as a kitten.
It is as glorious as a ballerina.
It is as pretty as a mermaid.
It is as lovely as a dolphin.
It is as beautiful as a pearl.
It is a flower.

Róisín Murphy (6)
Haselbury Plucknett CE First School, Haselbury

Untitled

It is as naughty as a robber.
It is as hot as an oven.
It is as loud as a radio.
It is as fast as a cheetah.
It is as brown as mud.
It is as rude as a parrot.
It is as cheeky as a monkey.
It is as funny as a clown.
It is a gingerbread man.

Ben French (6)
Haselbury Plucknett CE First School, Haselbury

Untitled

She is as beautiful as a butterfly.
She is as pretty as a princess.
She is as brown as a conker.
She is as soft as a sheep.
She is my new puppy.

Anna Kingston (5)
Haselbury Plucknett CE First School, Haselbury

Untitled

It is as springy as a kangaroo.
It is as slippery as a snake.
It is as blue as the sea.
It is as black as a tunnel.
It is as red as meat.
It is covered in cobwebs like a dungeon.
It is as big as a jeep.
It is as wide as a paddling pool.
It is my trampoline.

Jack Busby (6)
Haselbury Plucknett CE First School, Haselbury

Untitled

It is as massive as an elephant.
It is as loud as a helicopter.
It floats like a feather.
It is a Mexican shape.
It is as grey as a road.
It is Darth Vader's ship.

Charlie Lefeuvre (5)
Haselbury Plucknett CE First School, Haselbury

Untitled

They are as orange as a lion.
They are as white as a cloud.
They are as big as a rabbit.
They are as furry as a cat.
They are as naughty as a gorilla.
They are my guinea pigs.

Dean Thomas (5)
Haselbury Plucknett CE First School, Haselbury

Untitled

He is as brown as a cat.
He is as nice as a rabbit.
He is as loud as a cow.
He is as soft as a teddy bear.
He is as friendly as Charlie.
He is Hector, Ben's dog.

Ethan Gould
Haselbury Plucknett CE First School, Haselbury

Untitled

She is as beautiful as a butterfly.
She is as kind as God.
She is as lovely as Katie.
She is as pink as a flower.
She wears a crown.
She is a princess.

Catherine Hayton (5)
Haselbury Plucknett CE First School, Haselbury

It

It is as noisy as a hedge trimmer.
It is as red as a tongue.
It is as heavy as a house.
It is as shiny as glass.
It is as comfy as my bed.
It is my motorbike.

Harvey Coate (6)
Haselbury Plucknett CE First School, Haselbury

Untitled

He is as cute as a baby.
She is as beautiful as a mummy.
He is as good as a dog.
She is as bad as a bear.
He is as great as a bear.
She is as pretty as a princess.
They are my puppies.

Tia Holt (6)
Haselbury Plucknett CE First School, Haselbury

Untitled

I am as happy as Mary Poppins.
I am as excited as a hyena.
My dress is like sunshine.
My sash is as red as my car.
My wig is as black as a koala.
I am dressing up as Snow White.

Grace Bryant (5)
Haselbury Plucknett CE First School, Haselbury

Untitled

It is as green as grass.
It is as pink as a pig.
It is as purple as my unicorn.
It is as red as a rose.
It is as colourful as a parrot.
It is a rainbow.

Izabella Watts (5)
Haselbury Plucknett CE First School, Haselbury

Untitled

They are as black as night.
They are as soft as a teddy bear.
They are as ginger as sand.
They are as noisy as a gorilla.
They are my chickens.

Joseph Knight (5)
Haselbury Plucknett CE First School, Haselbury

Katie

She's as pretty as a flower,
She's as kind as can be,
She's as cheeky as a monkey,
Just like I can be.
She's a very special person,
I love her lots and lots,
She's the best cousin there could be,
She's my cousin, Katie.

Ellie-Jane Munro (6)
Holy Family RC Primary School, Oldham

He Is . . .

He is as cool as a cucumber.
He is as funny as a clown.
He is as friendly as my sister
And he is as brave as a lion.
He snacks like a monster.
He is my favourite cartoon.
He is the dog called Scooby-Doo.

Erin Fox (6)
Holy Family RC Primary School, Oldham

Harry

He's faster than a snail
He's cooler than a rat
He's smaller than a mouse
He gets lost in my house
He lives in his shell
He's brown like a bell
He's Harry, my tortoise.

Ethan Ian Grimes (6)
Holy Family RC Primary School, Oldham

He Is Fred, My Pet Ferret

He's as blind as a bat
He's as fluffy as a cat
He's as smelly as a rat
He's brown with beady eyes
Around his hutch there's lots of flies
He nips my ears and jumps on my feet
And for a treat, I give him raw meat
He lives in a straw bed
And his name is Fred
He's my pet ferret.

Amy Heywood-McGiffen (6)
Holy Family RC Primary School, Oldham

Famous Footballer

He comes from Spain,
He is very fast,
He is as quick as a lion,
He scores loads of goals,
He's Fernando Torres.

Lewis Fagan (7)
Holy Family RC Primary School, Oldham

Good And Naughty

They are as cute as a puppy
But as naughty as a baddy.
They like running away like a spider
And chasing like a dog.
They are big and small
And as funny as a clown.
They are best friends.
They are Tom and Jerry.

Joseph Jordan (6)
Holy Family RC Primary School, Oldham

Hannah Montana

She is as pretty as a butterfly
She is as strong as a bee
She is as pretty as a princess
She floats just like a leaf
She is a rock star
She is as famous as can be
She is loud
She is proud
She is everything to me
She is my hero
She is my star
She is my superstar
She is Hannah Montana.

Demi-Leigh Mycan (6)
Holy Family RC Primary School, Oldham

I Love My Dog

He is as furry as a rabbit,
He is as shiny as a jewel,
He is as nice as my daddy,
He is as big as a gate,
He is as dirty as a muddy puddle,
He is as soft as wool,
He is as funny as a clown.

He is Beau, my dog.

Madison Swailes (5)
Howard Primary School, Tamworth

Who Is She?

She is as lovely as a horse
She is as pretty as a picture
She is as shiny as a mirror
She is as bright as a button
She is friendly like me
She is as good as gold

She is Minnie Mouse.

Olivia Szwed (5)
Howard Primary School, Tamworth

My Horse, Flo

She's as cool as a cucumber
She's as cheeky as a monkey
She's as greedy as a pig
She's as wonderful as a sunflower
She's as bright as a button
She's as big as a bus
She is my horse, Flo.

Lorna Preece (5)
Howard Primary School, Tamworth

What Is He?

He has been told he is as big as a lorry.
He has a small mouth.
He has long eyelashes.
He has big ears.
He has four fat feet.
He has a smelly tail.
He is an elephant,
My favourite animal.

Charlie Simmonds (5)
Howard Primary School, Tamworth

Koala Bears

She is as snuggly buggly as a teddy bear.
She is as sweet as a peach.
She is as soft as my pussycat or mum.
She is like a butterfly.
She is as scared as a kitten.
She is a koala bear.

Eve Rich (6)
Langley Moor Primary School, Langley Moor

Pretty Peacocks

He is beautiful like a parrot
He is colourful like a clownfish
He is lovely like a cat
He is like a naughty monkey
He is like a feathery chick
He is like a wonderful dolphin.

He is a peacock.

Abby Bell (6)
Langley Moor Primary School, Langley Moor

Seals

She is as amazing as a plum
She is as cute as a dog
She is as gooey as a frog
She is as smelly as a swamp
She is as sloppy as a jelly
She is as cheeky as a monkey
She is a seal.

Megan Harris (6)
Langley Moor Primary School, Langley Moor

Simba

He's as fierce as a bear
He's as scruffy as a dog
He's as lazy as a cat
He's as bad a hyena
He's as orange as a monkey
He's as tall as a dog
He's as lovely as a rabbit
He's as fast as a cheetah
He's as scared as a kitten.
It's Simba.

Lily Local (6)
Langley Moor Primary School, Langley Moor

A Dog

He is as beautiful as a mum
He is hairy like a gorilla
He is furry like a cat
He is soft like a blanket
He is fluffy like a carpet
He is spiky like a hedgehog
He is naughty like a monkey
He is nice like a mam
It is a dog.

Adam Oyston (6)
Langley Moor Primary School, Langley Moor

A Dog

He is as thirsty as a gorilla.
He is as funny as a clown.
He is as good as a baby.
He is as dancy as a famous dancer.
He is as excited as a builder.
He is as speedy as a cheetah.
He is as terrified as a rock star.
He is scared like a girl.
He is a dog.

Jack Harris (6)
Langley Moor Primary School, Langley Moor

My Cat

He's as busy as a ball.
He's as funny as a clown.
He's as silly as a monkey.
He's as cheeky as a peacock.
He's as naughty as a lion.
He's as amazing as a superhero.
He's as fluffy as a bunny.
He's as lovely as my friend Anna.
He's as nice as Aimee, my friend.
He's as little as a bat.
He's as active as a wolf.
He's as lazy as a sloth.
He's as twitchy as the sun.
He's as smiley as my friend Megan.
He's as happy as Emma, my friend.
He's as helpful as Anna's dog, Yoonis.
He's Simba, my cat.

Lina Van Hunen (6)
Langley Moor Primary School, Langley Moor

Fantastic Lion

He is furry like a gorilla.
He is as colourful as a butterfly.
He is as fabulous as a monkey.
He is as brilliant as my friend.
He's a lion.

Livvy Dawson (7)
Langley Moor Primary School, Langley Moor

He Is A Cheetah

He is as cheeky as a clown.
He is as funny as a monkey.
He is as naughty as a gorilla.
He is as silly as a clown.
He is as fast as a tiger.
He is as fluffy as a dog.
He is as lovely as a cat.
He is as wonderful as a rat.
He is as amazing as a puppet.
He is a cheetah.

Ben Hindmarch (6)
Langley Moor Primary School, Langley Moor

A Cheeky Cat

She is as cuddly as my dog.
She is as soft as my teddy bear.
She is as summery as my dress.
She is a princess when she wears my crown.
She is as happy as my sister's smile.
She has as nice a tail as my dog.
She is as angelic as my cousin.
She is as lovely as my bed.
She's got a cheeky smile like my sister.
She is a cat.

Lucy Bradbury (6)
Langley Moor Primary School, Langley Moor

Hop, Hop, Hop

She is lovely like a flower
She is as cute as a cat
She is as pretty as a princess
She is as gorgeous as my teddy bear
She is excited like it is a party
She is as leapy as a frog
She is as happy as my mam
She is a bunny.

Megan Clark (6)
Langley Moor Primary School, Langley Moor

My Cheetah

He runs fast like a tiger.
He has spots everywhere on him.
He is as yellow as a sun.
He has a long tail like a monkey.
He is a cheetah.

Daniel Wilson (6)
Langley Moor Primary School, Langley Moor

My Dog

She is as happy as a princess.
She is as cheeky as can be.
She is as lovely as you.
She is as soft as a snail's body.
She is as cuddly as a bear.
She is a dog.

Bailey Ross (6)
Langley Moor Primary School, Langley Moor

Guinea Pig

He is as hungry as an alligator.
He is as cute as a puppy.
He is as noisy as a monkey.
He is as handsome as a prince.
He is as big as a teddy bear.
He is my guinea pig.

Kathryn Scrivens (6)
Langley Moor Primary School, Langley Moor

My Dog, Penny

She is as amazing as a cat.
She is as smiley as a horse.
She is as cheeky as a monkey.
She is as funny as an alien.
She is as cuddly as a blanket.
She is as naughty as me.
She is as sleepy as Simba.
She is Penny, my dog.

Emma Robinson (6)
Langley Moor Primary School, Langley Moor

Princess

She is as lovely as a puppy.
She is as soft as a sheep.
She is as lazy as a dog.
She is as funny as a clown.
She is as friendly as a pig.
She is as beautiful as a giraffe.
She is as cheeky as a monkey.
She is as pretty as an elephant.
She is as happy as a girl.
She is as black as a coat.
She is as cute as a mam.
She is a cat.

Sophie Parnaby (6)
Langley Moor Primary School, Langley Moor

Dogs Rock

She's as happy as a clown
She's as playful as a kitten
She's as soft as a sheep
She's as furry as a teddy
She's as fast as a train
She's as pretty as a princess
She's as warm as fire
She's as nice as a fairy
She's as cute as a flower
She's as golden as the sun
She's as helpful as the police
She's as cheeky as a monkey
She's as smooth as wool
She's as smiley as Lina, my friend
She's my dog, Unice.

Anna Lessels (6)
Langley Moor Primary School, Langley Moor

My Dog, Jess

She is as cheeky as a monkey.
She is scared of thunderstorms.
She is hungry all the time.
She is cute like an angel.
She is as brown as a bear.
She is silly like a clown.
She is soft like a teddy.
She is as little as a kitten.
She is my dog, Jess.

Lucy Newton (6)
Langley Moor Primary School, Langley Moor

A Cheetah

He's as hairy as a gorilla.
He's as spotty as a giraffe.
He's as fast as a T-rex.
He's as amazing as a gymnast.
He's as scary as a devil.
He's as cool as the best footballer in the world.
He's as wonderful as a teddy bear.
He's as furry as a little lamb.
Who is it?
He's a cheetah!

Mark Heron (6)
Langley Moor Primary School, Langley Moor

Guess Who?

She's as gorgeous as a teddy.
She's as fluffy as a flower.
She's as ginger as some wallpaper.
She's as soft as a pillow.
She's as lovely as a dog.
She's as black as a castle.
She's as brown as a kangaroo.
She's as cheeky as a monkey.
She's as smelly as a gorilla.
She's amazing like a giraffe.
She's a cat.

Aimee Liddy (6)
Langley Moor Primary School, Langley Moor

My Dog

He's as hairy as a gorilla.
He's as tall as a cat.
He's as happy as me.
He's as cheeky as a monkey.
He's as fierce as a lion.
He's as sad as a rat.
He's as fluffy as a pillow.
He's got pointy ears like a giraffe.
He's got patches like a guinea pig.
He's got the bushiest tail like a bush.
He's as nice as the police.
He's as naughty as my sister Molly.
It is my dog.

Max McKay (6)
Langley Moor Primary School, Langley Moor

My Riddle

I have four legs.
I am fluffy.
I like eating smelly fish.
I live with the lighthouse keeper.
I say *miaow!*

What am I?
Hamish, a lighthouse keeper's cat.

Bryluen Cowling (6)
Launceston CP School, Launceston

My Riddle

I have four legs and I'm greedy
I like fish
I live in a white cottage and I have a basket to sleep in
I am scared
I have ginger fur
I am scared of heights
It makes me seasick.

What am I?
Hamish the cat.

Harvey Cholwill (6)
Launceston CP School, Launceston

My Riddle

I have sharp teeth.
I have an endless tail.
I am a lighthouse keeper's pet.
I have blunt claws.
I like fish.

What am I?
Hamish the cat.

Harriet de Glanville (6)
Launceston CP School, Launceston

My Riddle

I have four legs and I am ginger.
I am as fluffy as a cushion.
I am lazy.
I eat tuna fish
And I miaow.

What am I?
Hamish the cat.

Maisie Hillon (6)
Launceston CP School, Launceston

My Riddle

I am a building
And I have wire going to the cottage.
I have a bright light flashing.
I am standing out to sea
And I am tall.

What am I?
A lighthouse.

Izaac Kirwan (7)
Launceston CP School, Launceston

My Riddle

I have four legs.
I am fluffy
And my eyes glow in the dark.

What am I?
A cat.

Ria Cardona (6)
Launceston CP School, Launceston

Silly Sausage

He's as silly as a sausage
He's as fluffy as a jumper
His ears are floppy
He's as jumpy as a grasshopper
He's my bunny, Flaky.

Madeleine Eldridge (8)
Lingfield Notre Dame School, Lingfield

Springer Spaniels

He's as sweet as a piece of chocolate
He's as playful as a bear
He's as cute as a cub
He's as cheeky as a monkey
He's my dog, Alfie.

Lulu Penton (6)
Lingfield Notre Dame School, Lingfield

Silly Sister, Phoebe

She is as clever as a cook
She is silly like a clown
She is as smart as a Smartie
She is as strong as a mop
She is as clever as a clog
She is my sister, Phoebe.

Saskia Bool (6)
Lingfield Notre Dame School, Lingfield

My Dad

He is as funny as a clown
He is as rich as a pop star
He is as cute as a cat
He is as clever as a teacher.

Jack Hearn (6)
Lingfield Notre Dame School, Lingfield

My Cat Toodles

He is as silly as me.
He is as naughty as a shark.
He is as funny as Daddy.
He is as lovely as his brother.
He is my cat, Toodles.

Isabella Dunsdon (5)
Lingfield Notre Dame School, Lingfield

Ashley Cole

He is as good as Simon Cowell
He is as sporty as a footballer
He is as good as a dog
He is as friendly as a deer
He is Ashley Cole.

Matthew Holm (6)
Lingfield Notre Dame School, Lingfield

Untitled

He is as kind as a friend.
He is as nice as a flower.
He is as helpful as a girl.
He is as solid as a gran.
He is as lovely as a teddy.
He is my dog called Bouncer.

Lucy Wallis Bullock (5)
Lingfield Notre Dame School, Lingfield

He

He is as lovely as a love heart.
He is as cuddly as a teddy.
He is as nice as chocolate.
He is as funny as a clown.
He is as cute as me.
He is as cheeky as a monkey.
He is my cousin, George.

Emily Leeves (5)
Lingfield Notre Dame School, Lingfield

Untitled

He is as nice as a mum
He is as kind as a nan
He is as helpful as a teacher
He is my friend, Joe.

Marko Wirya Sepulveda (5)
Lingfield Notre Dame School, Lingfield

She

She is as pretty as a princess.
She is as talented as Cheryl Cole.
She is as good as a pop star.
She is as lovely as a love heart.
She is as good as a real dancer.
She is as famous as Michael Jackson.
She is Hannah Montana.

Aysha McCrossen (5)
Lingfield Notre Dame School, Lingfield

Untitled

He is as nice as a pirate
He is as funny as a clown
He is as good as a queen
He is as scary as a shark
He is Sebastian Perkins, my friend.

Joe Jolliffe (5)
Lingfield Notre Dame School, Lingfield

She

She is as clever as an artist
She is as kind as a nurse
She is as lovely as a flower
She is as beautiful as a princess
She is as cute as my teddy
She is my mummy.

Eve Ozmen (5)
Lingfield Notre Dame School, Lingfield

Eve

She is as kind as my mummy
She is as nice as my sister
She is as friendly as my teacher
She is as beautiful as a princess
She is my best friend, Eve.

Michaela O'Neill (5)
Lingfield Notre Dame School, Lingfield

Emma

She is as happy as a butterfly
She is as good as a princess
She is as nice as a dog
She is Emma, my sister.

William Huddleston (6)
Lingfield Notre Dame School, Lingfield

Jerry

He is as funny as a clown.
He is as cheeky as a monkey.
He is as furry as a brown cat.
He runs as fast as a cheetah.
His tail is as long as a cat's tail.
He is Jerry from Tom and Jerry.

Sophia McInnes (6)
Lingfield Notre Dame School, Lingfield

Darcey Bussell

Her ballet suit is as white as a diamond.
Her moves are as good as the sun.
She is as beautiful as a butterfly.
Her ballet is as fast as a cheetah.
She is Darcey Bussell.

Sophie Lee (6)
Lingfield Notre Dame School, Lingfield

Hannah Montana

She is as pretty as a sparkly diamond.
She sings like a robin.
Her eyes are as shiny as a silver coin.
She is as colourful as a rainbow.
She is Hannah Montana.

Hannah Jones (6)
Lingfield Notre Dame School, Lingfield

Wayne Rooney

He is as fast as a cheetah.
His kick is as powerful as a boot.
He is as cool as a cucumber.
He is as strong as a crane.
He is as bald as Shrek.
He is Wayne Rooney.

Oliver Greenfield (6)
Lingfield Notre Dame School, Lingfield

Louie

As funny as a clown.
As kind as a monkey.
As strong as a skeleton.
As magic as a pumpkin.
He is my brother.

Leo Steel (6)
Lingfield Notre Dame School, Lingfield

Hannah Montana

She sings like a robin.
Her eyes are like twinkling stars.
She's as pretty as a butterfly.
Her dress is like glittery sparkles.
Her hair is like feathers.
I think she's the best singer in town.
She is Hannah Montana.

Tabitha Hughes (6)
Lingfield Notre Dame School, Lingfield

Roald Dahl

He is as awesome as his books.
He is as clever as a teacher.
He has good ideas like a hard worker.
He is as old as you can get.
He is better than my best friend.
He is Roald Dahl.

Caitlin Birchall (6)
Lingfield Notre Dame School, Lingfield

Wayne Rooney

He can run as fast as a cheetah.
He is as sweaty as a shark.
He is as powerful as a house.
His hair is spiky like a zebra.
He is cheeky like a monkey.
He is Wayne Rooney.

Mark Mitchell (6)
Lingfield Notre Dame School, Lingfield

Queen Elizabeth II

She is as kind as my best friend
She is as pretty as a golden peacock feather
She's as colourful as a butterfly.
She is as famous as Peter Andre.
She smells like lavender.
She is the Queen.

Holly Cooper (6)
Lingfield Notre Dame School, Lingfield

David Beckham

He runs as fast as a cheetah
He is as cool as a pop star
He is as famous as Wayne Rooney
He kicks as hard as an erupting volcano
He is as strong as a crane
He is David Beckham.

Finley Perkins (6)
Lingfield Notre Dame School, Lingfield

Jerry Mouse

He is as fast as a leopard.
He is better than my mum.
He is as quiet as an ant.
He is as clever as a scientist.
He is as funny as a clown.
He is a better hider than someone lost in a maze.
He is Jerry Mouse.

Max Godwin (6)
Lingfield Notre Dame School, Lingfield

Hannah Montana

She is as wonderful and beautiful as an angel.
Her dress sways like waves or ships sent out to sea.
Her hair is like a web that is golden.
Her eyes shine like gleaming crystals.
She is the best singer in town.
She is Hannah Montana!

Sophia Bernau (6)
Lingfield Notre Dame School, Lingfield

Hannah Montana

She sparkles like lots of crystals.
She is as pretty as an angel fish.
She is the best actor in the world.
Her eyes sparkle like diamonds.
She sings like an angel.
She is Hannah Montana.

Grace Carney (7)
Lingfield Notre Dame School, Lingfield

Simon Cowell

His hair is as flat as a pancake
He is as beautiful as a glistening star
He is famous for being on TV
He is X Factor
He is Simon Cowell.

Brooke Whittell (6)
Lingfield Notre Dame School, Lingfield

Cristiano Ronaldo

He is as fast as a leopard chasing a hare.
He's as famous as the sun.
He is as strong as an elephant.
He is Cristiano Ronaldo.

Luke Holland (6)
Lingfield Notre Dame School, Lingfield

Eddie Murphy

He is as funny as a joke book.
He is as stupid as a squirrel.
He is as hairy as a gorilla.
His hooves in Shrek look like horses' hooves.
He is Eddie Murphy.

Esme Hedges (6)
Lingfield Notre Dame School, Lingfield

My Daddy

He is as funny as a clown
He is as clever as a teacher
He is as fast as a rocket
He is my racing daddy.

Ella Taylor (5)
Lingfield Notre Dame School, Lingfield

Max

He is as funny as a clown
He is as good as a football
He is as fast as a rocket
He is as scary as a dinosaur
He is as cuddly as a teddy
He is Max, my brother.

Kian Cooper (5)
Lingfield Notre Dame School, Lingfield

Isabel

She is as funny as a monkey.
She is as lovely as a flower.
She is as kind as a sister.
She is as clever as an owl.
She is my friend, Isabel.

Flori Kimber (5)
Lingfield Notre Dame School, Lingfield

My Friend, Matthew

Faster than a Ferrari.
Faster than a cheetah.
Faster than a horse.
Faster than a train.
My friend, Matthew.

William Oakeby (5)
Lingfield Notre Dame School, Lingfield

My Daddy

He is as nice as a sweet
He is as funny as a clown
He is as fast as a lion
He is as cool as a footballer
He is as kind as a flower
He is my daddy.

Nathan O'Neilll (5)
Lingfield Notre Dame School, Lingfield

Freddie

He is faster than a jet.
He is as cool as an owl.
He is as nice as a koala.
It is Freddie.

Charlie Williams (5)
Lingfield Notre Dame School, Lingfield

John

Funny as an elephant.
Naughty as a cheetah.
Clever as a giraffe.
He is my friend, John.

Edward Godwin (5)
Lingfield Notre Dame School, Lingfield

My Mummy

Pretty as a rainbow
Kind as a flower
Cuddly as a rabbit
Helpful as an elephant
She is my mummy.

Tom Bailey (5)
Lingfield Notre Dame School, Lingfield

Thumper

He is as cuddly as a koala.
He is as soft as a cloud.
He is as cute as a giraffe.
He is my teddy.

Sebastian Perkins (5)
Lingfield Notre Dame School, Lingfield

Charlotte

She is as funny as a clown.
She is as cuddly as a teddy.
She is as pretty as a parrot.
She is as clever as a horse
She is my friend, Charlotte.

Christina O'Neilll (5)
Lingfield Notre Dame School, Lingfield

My Brother, Joe

He is as fast as a jet.
He is as feisty as a crab.
He is as silly as a pear.
He is my brother, Joe.

Jules Jardim (6)
Lingfield Notre Dame School, Lingfield

Puppies

It is as cute as a bird.
It is as fluffy as a fur ball.
It is as cuddly as a teddy.
It is as lovely as a rose.
It is as sweet as a buttercup.
It is a puppy.

Nancy Lee McAlister (7)
Lingfield Notre Dame School, Lingfield

He Likes . . .

He likes CBeebies like my cousin.
He loves it when I chase him like a dog.
He loves going out like a monkey.
He likes chocolate like Miss Read.
He loves cars like Josh.
He is Zach.

Grace Hutchings (6)
Marden Primary School, Marden

He . . .

He wears gloves like a gardener.
He breathes like an astronaut.
He is as young as Darth Maul.
He is as well known as Roald Dahl.
He's as powerful as a tongue twister.
He's Darth Vader.

Rowan Galler (7)
Marden Primary School, Marden

Untitled

He is good at football
He is good at back flicking
He is Steven Gerrard.

Owen Orpin (6)
Marden Primary School, Marden

Untitled

She is good at making cakes
She is good at tickling me like a caterpillar.
When I have hurt myself she always makes me better.
She loves me lots like Daddy.
She is as tall as a giraffe.
She likes putting make-up on like a make-up model.
She has got long eyelashes.
It is Mummy!

Maisie Lilley (7)
Marden Primary School, Marden

Guess Who?

He is cool
He can play football
He is silly
His name is Matt Smith.

Bradley Edwards (6)
Marden Primary School, Marden

Uncle Kev

He is as cool as a star.
He is as cool as a giraffe.
He is as cool as a rock.
He is as cool as a zombie.
He is as cool as a pen.
He is as cool as a Porsche.
He is as cool as a sticker.
He is Uncle Kevan.

Rebecca Rosario (7)
Marden Primary School, Marden

My Friend

She has curly hair and brown eyes
And a red tongue.
She loves the colour blue.
She has long hair.
She is Evie!

Alice Mantle (6)
Marden Primary School, Marden

Untitled

She is as nice as a flower.
She likes to swim.
She is a mermaid when she swims.
She is as soft as a flower.
It is my friend, Daisy.

Millie Phillips (6)
Marden Primary School, Marden

Untitled

He is as clever as a computer.
He is as tall as a tower.
He is as happy as a monkey.
He is as fast as a horse.
He is my daddy!

Callum Benson (6)
Marden Primary School, Marden

Untitled

He is as cute as a teddy bear.
He is as cuddly as a pillow.
He is as lovely as a flower.
He is as soft as a flower.
It is my brother, Billy.

Daisy Moss (6)
Marden Primary School, Marden

Untitled

He has cute hair like a stylish monkey.
He is always by my side.
We are best friends.
His favourite game is football.
He is my best friend, George.

Matthew Wareham (7)
Marden Primary School, Marden

Untitled

Kind like a button.
Brown hat, lovely shoes.
Sparkly like a diamond.
Nice as a person.
It is Daisy, my friend.

Rebecca Watling (6)
Marden Primary School, Marden

My Brother

He swims as fast as a shark.
He is as arty as an artist.
He is as cool as a rock star.
He is as tall as a horse.
He is as clever as me.
He is my brother, Sebastian.

Casper Munro-Smith (6)
Moreton Hall Prep School, Bury St Edmunds

My Dog

He is as fast as a cheetah.
He is as jumpy as a kangaroo.
He is as funny as a clown.
He is as grey as my pencil.
He is my dog, Blake.

Ishtar Loft (6)
Moreton Hall Prep School, Bury St Edmunds

My Daddy

He is as kind as a king.
He is as funny as a clown.
He is as tall as a tree.
He is as strong as a circus strong man.
He is as happy as a gingerbread man.
He is my daddy.

Millie Gale (6)
Moreton Hall Prep School, Bury St Edmunds

My Cat, Baloo

He is as cuddly as a bear.
He is as young as me.
He is as white as paper.
He is as soft as a bunny.
He is the best in the world.
He is my cat, Baloo.

Eloise Forbes (6)
Moreton Hall Prep School, Bury St Edmunds

My Friend, Rozina

She is as nice as a rose.
She is as happy as a hamster.
She is as cheeky as a monkey.
She is as funny as a clown.
She is as cute as a puppy.
She is my friend, Rozina.

Myrah Ahmed (6)
Moreton Hall Prep School, Bury St Edmunds

My Dog

He is as naughty as a clown.
He is as soft as a cloud.
He is as soft as a teddy bear.
He is as fast as a train.
He is my dog.

Ellis Lloyd (5)
Nonsuch Primary School, Woodgate Valley

My Cat

He is as naughty as a gorilla.
He is as spotty as a cheetah.
He is as soft as a teddy bear.
He is as fast as a car.
He is as cute as a baby.
He is my cat.

Harrison Baker (5)
Nonsuch Primary School, Woodgate Valley

Jedee

He is as hungry as a cat.
He hides well as an agent.
He is as good as a friend.
He is as good as money.
He swims as fast as a man in a race.
He is my pet goldfish.

Aaron Ray Bondoc (5)
Nonsuch Primary School, Woodgate Valley

Pink

She is as soft as a blanket.
She is as stripy as a zebra.
She is as cute as a teddy bear.
She is as orange as a Satsuma.
She is as warm as the sun.
She is my toy tiger, Pink.

Charlie Woodward (6)
Nonsuch Primary School, Woodgate Valley

My Cat

He is as soft as a cloud
He is as funny as a clown
He is as cute as a dog
He is as hungry as a child
He is as silly as an elephant
He is my cat.

Daniel Donovan (5)
Nonsuch Primary School, Woodgate Valley

Friend Riddle

He is as fast as Wayne Rooney.
He is as funny as a clown.
He is as cheeky as a monkey.
He is as tall as the Eiffel Tower.
He is as naughty as a 2-year-old.
He is as strong as the Undertaker.
He is Roan, my friend.

Danny Seton (6)
Rothbury First School, Rothbury

Roan's Riddle

He is as nice as a dolphin
He is as good as the Prime Minister
He is as helpful as a servant
He is as great as an ice cream man
He is as tall as a goal post
He is as happy as a party person
He is Torres.

Roan Stripp (6)
Rothbury First School, Rothbury

Untitled

Her neck is as tall as a tree.
Her legs are as long as a ladder.
Her tongue is as black as coal.
Her ears are as small as a ball.
Her eyelashes are as long as some grass.
Her eyes are as blue as the sea.
She is a giraffe.

Grace Howson (6)
Rothbury First School, Rothbury

The Magic Riddle

He is as magic as a wizard.
His eyes twinkle like stars.
He is as kind as God.
He is as good as Professor Brainstorm.
He is as friendly as Toy Story Ralph.
He is as brave as a dragon.
He is Merlin.

Samuel Ewen (6)
Rothbury First School, Rothbury

Untitled

He is as fast as a bullet
He is as tall as the Eiffel Tower
He is as rich as the Queen
He is as nice as a lie in
He is Steven Gerrard.

Elliott Fox (6)
Rothbury First School, Rothbury

The Nasty Riddle

As scary as a monster.
It bites turtle shells.
It kills people for food.
As bad as a devil.
Swims as fast as a jaguar.
Eats fish when it's hungry.
It's a shark.

Ewan Williams (7)
Rothbury First School, Rothbury

My Mum

She is as pink as a pig.
She is as pretty as the cats.
She is as kind as the sun.
She is my mum.

Finlay Willson (5)
St Francis Xavier's RC Primary School, Hereford

God

He is as powerful as electricity.
He can see everything like night vision.
He is as helpful as a doctor.
He is as caring as a mother.
He is as wonderful as a flower.
He guides us like a map.
He is God.

Jessica Thompson (7)
St Francis Xavier's RC Primary School, Hereford

My Mum

She is stronger than a dinosaur.
She is louder than a lion.
She is as funny as a monkey.
She is my mum.

Tom Thomas (5)
St Francis Xavier's RC Primary School, Hereford

My Dog

She is as kind as a rabbit.
She is as soft as a sheep.
She is as furry as a cat.
She is as lovely as a zebra.
She is as funny as a clown.
She is my dog.

Jack Summerfield (5)
St Francis Xavier's RC Primary School, Hereford

Simon Cowell

He is harder than a piece of wood.
He is as famous as a pop star.
He is as clever as a clown.
He is as handsome as a pig.
He is as bossy as a pilot.
He is Simon Cowell.

Natalie Vaughan (7)
St Francis Xavier's RC Primary School, Hereford

Santa Claus

He is as greedy as a pig.
He has boots as black as soot.
He is as fat as a whale.
He has a big hat like a rock.
He has a long beard like a stick.
He can fly like a bird.
He is as fast as a cheetah.
He is Santa Claus.

Millie Beecham (6)
St Francis Xavier's RC Primary School, Hereford

God

He is as strong as a python.
He is as scary as a dragon.
He is as long as a crocodile.
He is as wonderful as the world.
He is as hungry as a horse.
He is as nice as a mouse.
He is as happy as a bear.
He is as funny as a monkey.
He is God.

Harvey Bennett (6)
St Francis Xavier's RC Primary School, Hereford

Bear

He is as fast as a tiger.
He is as big as a tree.
He is as loud as a lion.
He is as furry as a rabbit.
He is as scary as a dinosaur.
He is as nice as my mum.
He is a bear.

Pedro De Sousa Tindall (6)
St Francis Xavier's RC Primary School, Hereford

Rabbit

She is as soft as a blanket.
She is as grey as a rhinoceros.
She is as nice as a mum.
She hops like a kangaroo.
She twitches like a cat.
She eats lots of carrots.
She has a long tail.
She is as cute as a dog.
She is a rabbit.

Monique Crombie (6)
St Francis Xavier's RC Primary School, Hereford

Thomas Edison

He is good at inventing.
His suit is as brown as trees.
His hat is as black as metal.
His inventions lit up the world.
He lived in a factory that's brown.
He worked hard like a lion.
His shoes are as black as charcoal.
He is Thomas Edison.

Alan Thankachan (7)
St Francis Xavier's RC Primary School, Hereford

Cheryl Cole

She is as beautiful as a flower.
She is as rich as a banker.
She is as bossy as a farmer.
She is as funny as a clown.
She is nicer than an elephant.
She sings like a bird.
She is Cheryl Cole.

Alice Pritchard (7)
St Francis Xavier's RC Primary School, Hereford

My Brother

He is as bright as the sun.
His hair is like silk.
He is as chubby as cheeks.
His eyelashes are long and sparkly.
He is active like a monkey.
He is my brother.

Megan Llewellyn (7)
St Francis Xavier's RC Primary School, Hereford

Untitled

She is as beautiful as flowers.
She is as nice as a teacher.
She has a crown like a princess.
She has a royal chair.
She has a royal stick.
She has a royal cloak.
She is the queen.

Olivia West (6)
St Francis Xavier's RC Primary School, Hereford

Untitled

She is funny like a clown
She is as pretty as a cat
She is as helpful as my grandad
She is as nice as my guinea pigs
She is my mummy.

Katie Parker (5)
St Francis Xavier's RC Primary School, Hereford

My Favourite Thing

It's my favourite toy
It's so tidy and clean
It's full of my friends
It's open all day
It's closed all night
It's pretty as a picture
It's my doll's house.

Leah Newton (5)
St Michael's Primary & Nursery School, Moodiesburn

A Coat

I have a zip.
I sometimes have buttons.
I have a hole at the top.
I have pockets.
I have holes on the sides for your arms.
I can keep you warm
I am a . . . coat.

Caitlyn Flynn (6)
St Stephen's CE Primary School, Kearsley

A Sunflower

I need water.
I need love.
I have petals.
I can grow in the sun.
I am a . . . sunflower.

Callum Paisley (6)
St Stephen's CE Primary School, Kearsley

A Coat

I keep you warm in winter.
I live on you.
I have pockets.
I am a . . . coat.

Jaicianna Deveney (6)
St Stephen's CE Primary School, Kearsley

A Snake

I live in the wild.
I have a tongue as red as a tin of tomato soup.
I am so scary you cannot believe your eyes.
I have black, dull spots.
I love to eat rats.
I am a . . . snake.

Jessica Stowell (6)
St Stephen's CE Primary School, Kearsley

A Coat

I slide on a hanger.
I have buttons on me.
I have pockets.
I go out.
I am a . . . coat.

Abigail Porter (6)
St Stephen's CE Primary School, Kearsley

A Bonfire

I am as hot as the sun.
I blow out flames and children run away from them.
I have logs to help me start.
I keep you warm when you are cold.
I am there at camping.
I am a . . . bonfire.

Isabel Hannon (6)
St Stephen's CE Primary School, Kearsley

A Spaceship

I zoom into the air.
I go higher than the clouds.
I have fire coming out of my tail.
I take brave astronauts up into space with me.
I see all the aliens in the world.

Megan Taylor (6)
St Stephen's CE Primary School, Kearsley

A Flower

I need water to help me grow.
I could be pink, yellow or any other colour.
I am as pretty as the sun.
I can have ten petals.
I can grow in everyone's garden.
I am a . . . flower.

Faith Hird (6)
St Stephen's CE Primary School, Kearsley

A Bonfire

I am boiling hot.
I need sticks to help set me on fire.
I am nice and warm.
I am a . . . bonfire.

Emi-Lee Bracegirdle (6)
St Stephen's CE Primary School, Kearsley

A Bonfire

I have red and orange flames.
I have wood at the bottom of me.
I make crackling noises.
I have people watching me.
I am a . . . bonfire.

Jack Weatherby (6)
St Stephen's CE Primary School, Kearsley

A Snake

I slide around people's necks.
I eat nice, hairy mice.
I live in the jungle.
I have a long red tongue.
I am a . . . snake.

Thomas Dickens (6)
St Stephen's CE Primary School, Kearsley

A Monster

I am as hairy as a lion.
I am as silly as a clown.
I am as scary as a vampire.
I can be as little as a finger.
I can be as wide as a person.
I am as wild as a tiger.
I am a . . . monster.

Nathaniel Campion (6)
St Stephen's CE Primary School, Kearsley

A Snake

It's as colourful as a colourful line.
It's as slimy as a worm.
It's as shiny as a frog.
It's as shiny as a rocket.
It's a snake.

Abby Mort (6)
St Stephen's CE Primary School, Kearsley

A Castle

It's as big as a mountain
It's as big as a giant
It's as tall as a tree
It's as long as a giraffe's neck
It's as big as a cloud
It's as grey as a thundercloud
It's as big as a school
It's as massive as a moon
It's a castle.

Sia Raw (6)
St Stephen's CE Primary School, Kearsley

A Beautiful Castle

It's as beautiful as a flower
It's as big as a giant
It's as long as a giraffe's neck
It's a big beautiful castle.

Constance Roe-Morton (5)
St Stephen's CE Primary School, Kearsley

A Dinosaur

It's as hard as a brick
It's as scaly as a dragon
It's as fierce as a crocodile
It's as big as a giant
It's a dinosaur.

Callum Wood (5)
St Stephen's CE Primary School, Kearsley

A Mountain

It's as big as a dinosaur
It's as rough as a branch
It's as hard as a rock
It's as snowy as the North Pole
It's a mountain.

Branden Green McCulloch (5)
St Stephen's CE Primary School, Kearsley

A Castle

It's as strong as a house
It's as big as a tower
It's as strong as a mountain
It's as pink as pink paint
It's a pink castle.

Isobel Fairhurst (5)
St Stephen's CE Primary School, Kearsley

A Castle

It's as massive as a church
It's as good as a rainbow
It's as tall as a house
It's as lovely as a flower
It's as grey as a rhino
It's a castle.

Caitlin Palmer (5)
St Stephen's CE Primary School, Kearsley

A Rocket

It's as shiny as a star
It's as fast as Sonic the Hedgehog
It's a rocket.

Callum Jones (5)
St Stephen's CE Primary School, Kearsley

A Castle

It's as hard as a rock
It's as tall as a giraffe's neck
It's as strong as a brick
It's a castle.

Georgia Brankley (5)
St Stephen's CE Primary School, Kearsley

A Monster

It's as scary as a dinosaur
It's as green as grass
It's a *monster.*

Louie Carruthers (5)
St Stephen's CE Primary School, Kearsley

143

A Rocket

It's as shiny as a star
It's as hard as a rock
It's as fast as a firework
It's a rocket.

Bobby McLellan (5)
St Stephen's CE Primary School, Kearsley

A Flower

It's as beautiful as it can be
It's as pretty as a butterfly
It's as smelly as perfume
It's a flower.

Jessica Murphy (5)
St Stephen's CE Primary School, Kearsley

A Rocket

It's as supersonic as a jet
It's as fast as it can be
It's as shiny as a Lamborghini
It's as expensive as an aeroplane
It's as heavy as a plane
It's a rocket.

Busankosi Ngubane (5)
St Stephen's CE Primary School, Kearsley

Fuzzy Head

I have green fuzzy hair
A long pointy body
With lots of wrinkles
I am bright orange
And I live in the mud.
What am I? A carrot!

Elise Gallagher (5)
The Highway Primary School, Orpington

He's White And Grey

He sleeps all day, he's white and grey.
He's quick and clever, I could stroke him forever
He always lands on his feet, he's so sweet
He is as greedy as can be, he really loves me
He likes to play and always get his way
He bit my mum, he can lick his tum
He scratches my door and opens it with his paw
We bought him a mat and he really likes that
I love Gizmo, my cat.

Elissa Cook (6)
The Highway Primary School, Orpington

Pooh Bear

He is very cuddly
He keeps my bed warm
He makes me happy when I cry
He goes everywhere with me
He is quite small
He is my best friend
He never walks off
He is Pooh Bear, my lovely toy.

Holly Elgy (5)
The Highway Primary School, Orpington

She Is?

She is beautiful
She is pretty
She looks after me
She gives me cuddles
She gives me kisses
She tucks me in my bed
She looks after me when I hurt myself
She is my mummy, I love her.

Megan Maryan (6)
The Highway Primary School, Orpington

Edward's Riddle

She is faster than a deer
She is as bouncy as me
She's as furry as a fox
Her ears are as silky as a dolphin's fin
Her eyes are as dark as a puddle
Her tail is as waggy as a flag in the wind
Her paws are as damp as the mist
She jumps up like a rabbit
Her fur is as black as the night sky
She is Lola, my puppy.

Edward Perry (5)
The New Beacon School, Sevenoaks

My Mystery Guest

He is as sweet as a mango
He is as scary as a lion
He is as fast as a cheetah
He is as funny as a monkey
He is as clever as a scientist
He is my best friend Henry.

Leonardo Bezuidenhout (5)
The New Beacon School, Sevenoaks

A Star Of The Wars

His ears are like an elf's,
His tunic tickles the floor,
He has bags under his eyes,
His green lightsaber flashes like lightning,
His walking stick is used as a weapon,
He has won against the emperor,
He has got The Force,
I wish he was real because he is the best,
He is Yoda.

James King (6)
The New Beacon School, Sevenoaks

Drake's First Riddle

He's as small as a beanbag
He's as smart as a fox
He's as strong as ever
He's as sweet as candyfloss
He's as fast as a Ferrari
He's as excited as a jumping silly horse
He's as cuddly as a teddy bear
He's my puppy, Drake.

Aidan Wood (5)
The New Beacon School, Sevenoaks

Who Is He?

He's as tall as a tower
He's better than a horse
He can run really fast
He's the best at sports
He's my dad!

Louis Day (6)
The New Beacon School, Sevenoaks

The Football Riddle

He's as tall as a tree
He's as fast as a cheetah
He's as solid as a house
He's as strong as an axe
He's as cunning as a fox
He is Peter Crouch.

Samuel Ford (6)
The New Beacon School, Sevenoaks

Grandpa Bill

He's as old as Mummy and Daddy stuck together,
He's as wise as a library,
He's as sporty as a football,
He's as playful as a puppy,
He's as fierce as a hunting dog,
He's as kind as Jesus,
He's my grandpa - Grandpa Bill - and he's 90 today!

Sam Foss (6)
The New Beacon School, Sevenoaks

My Superhero

He is as clever as an owl
He is as strong as a lion
And can lift me up to the sky
He is as funny as a clown
He is as cheeky as a monkey
He is faster than a cheetah
When he rides his bike
He is my daddy.

Theodore Collingwood (7)
The New Beacon School, Sevenoaks

Smiley Baby

She is as wriggly as an earthworm
She is as giggly as me
She is as strong as a superhero
She is as playful as a kitten
She is as warm as the sun
She is as noisy as a firework
She is as amazing as a rainbow
She is Naomi, my baby sister.

Elliot Wright (5)
The New Beacon School, Sevenoaks

My Brother

He eats like a chimp.
He loves me.
He never plays with me.
He always plays football.
He goes to Pannit Park all the time.
He is my brother, Luke.

Daisy Stokoe (6)
West Cliff Primary School, Whitby

My Teddy Bear

She is as cuddly as a bunny
She is as bossy as my mummy
She is as beautiful as Daddy
She is a girl
She has fat ears
She is my teddy.

Sidonie Inglis (6)
West Cliff Primary School, Whitby

My Pet Puppy

He is a cheeky monkey
He's as cute as a bunny
I love him
He has a long swinging tail
He is brown
He has eyes
He is my pet puppy.

Jessica Price (6)
West Cliff Primary School, Whitby

He

My dad is strong and fast.
He is daft.
He takes me to school.
He looks after me
He plays with me.
I love my dad.

Billy Cattermole (6)
West Cliff Primary School, Whitby

My Dad

He's as strong as an elephant.
He is as nice as God
He is as fun as a parrot
He is as fast as a cheetah
He is as lovely as Jesus
He's as cosy as a blanket
He's as friendly as a nice person
He loves TV
He loves custard
He likes working at his work with his friends
He loves seeing me
He is my dad!

Annaliese Querns (6)
West Cliff Primary School, Whitby

My Dad

He is fast
And as strong as a hippo
He is funny.
He is silly.
He likes Coke.
He is as comfy as a pillow.
He is a nice bed to sleep on!
He is my dad.

Mollie Burnett (6)
West Cliff Primary School, Whitby

The Cat

She is as fluffy as a rabbit.
She is faster than a cheetah.
She is cuter than a hamster.
She is a good girl.
She is hungry every day.
She is very fantastic.
She is wonderful.
She is a cat.

Marshall Kelly (6)
West Cliff Primary School, Whitby

Young Writers Information

We hope you have enjoyed reading this book - and that you will continue to enjoy it in the coming years.
If you like reading and writing poetry drop us a line, or give us a call, and we'll send you a free information pack.
Alternatively if you would like to order further copies of this book or any of our other titles, then please give us a call or log onto our website at www.youngwriters.co.uk.

Young Writers Information
Remus House
Coltsfoot Drive
Peterborough
PE2 9BF
(01733) 890066